CITY

CITY

A Story of Roman Planning and Construction

DAVID MACAULAY

COLLINS ST JAMES'S PLACE, LONDON

For Janice
and things to come

special thanks to Hardu, Mary,
Sidney, Bill, the old folks back
home, Melanie, Walter and Vitruvius.

First published by Houghton Mifflin Company Boston, U.S.A., 1974
First published in Great Britain 1975
The paperback edition first published in Great Britain 1982
Copyright © David Macaulay 1974

ISBN 0 00 192143 6 (paperback)
ISBN 0 00 192151 7 (hardback)

Made and printed in Great Britain by
William Collins Sons and Co Ltd Glasgow

By 200 B.C. soldiers of the Roman Republic had conquered all of Italy except the Alps. In the following three hundred years they created an empire extending from Spain to the Persian Gulf. To insure their hold over these lands the Roman soldiers built permanent military camps. As the need for military force lessened, many camps became important cities of the Roman Empire. The Romans knew that well planned cities did more to maintain peace and security than twice the number of military camps. They also knew that a city was more than just a business, government, or religious centre. It was all three, but most important, it had to be a place where people wanted to live.

Because cities were built either where no city previously existed or where a small village stood, the maximum population and size were determined before construction began. The planners then allotted adequate space for houses, shops, squares, and temples. They decided how much water would be needed and the number and size of streets, pavements, and sewers. By planning this way they tried to satisfy the needs of every individual — rich and poor alike.

The planners agreed that when a city reached its maximum population a new city should be built elsewhere. They recognized the danger of overpopulation. A city forced to grow beyond its walls not only burdened the existing water, sewage, and traffic systems but eventually destroyed the farmland on whose crops the people depended.

Although Verbonia is imaginary, its planning and construction are based on those of the hundreds of Roman cities founded between 300 B.C. and A.D. 150. No matter what brought about their creation, they were designed and built to serve the needs of all the people who lived within them. This kind of planning is the basis of any truly successful city. The need for it today is greater than ever.

For almost two hundred years the wheat and grapes of northern Italy's fertile Po Valley had been collected in small trading villages and shipped to Rome. In 26 B.C. a disastrous spring flood destroyed the villages along the Po riverbanks as well as an important bridge. When news reached the Emperor Augustus he immediately dispatched to the stricken area forty-five military engineers, including planners, architects, surveyors, and construction specialists. They were to supervise the building of a new bridge and new roads and to lay plans for a new city. The city was named Verbonia, and – in honour of the Emperor — Augusta Verbonia.

Augustus hoped to combine all the remaining trading villages into one secure and efficient trading center and so increase the amount of produce coming into Rome. To speed up development of the new city, he retired to the area two thousand soldiers, who would not only help build Verbonia but also become its first citizens.

First the surveyors selected the place where the city would be built. They chose a flat but sloping site (to insure good drainage) that was high enough to avoid future floods. A Roman priest examined the livers of a rabbit and a pheasant from the area to find out if it would be a healthy place in which to live. When the animals were found to be without fault and an investigation of the land turned up no stagnant pools, the gods were thanked and the choice of the site was officially confirmed.

The soldiers and the slaves who travelled with them then set up a military camp called a castrum. First they dug a protective ditch and erected a stockade fence around a rectangular area. Next the two main streets were marked off — one running from north to south, the other from east to west. They crossed at right angles above a long open space called the forum where the soldiers would gather daily to receive their orders. At one end of the forum the commander's tent was pitched. The tents for soldiers, slaves, and supplies filled the remainder of the castrum and were grouped in rows. In the following months all the tents were replaced by more permanent wooden shelters and a temporary bridge was constructed over boats anchored side by side across the river.

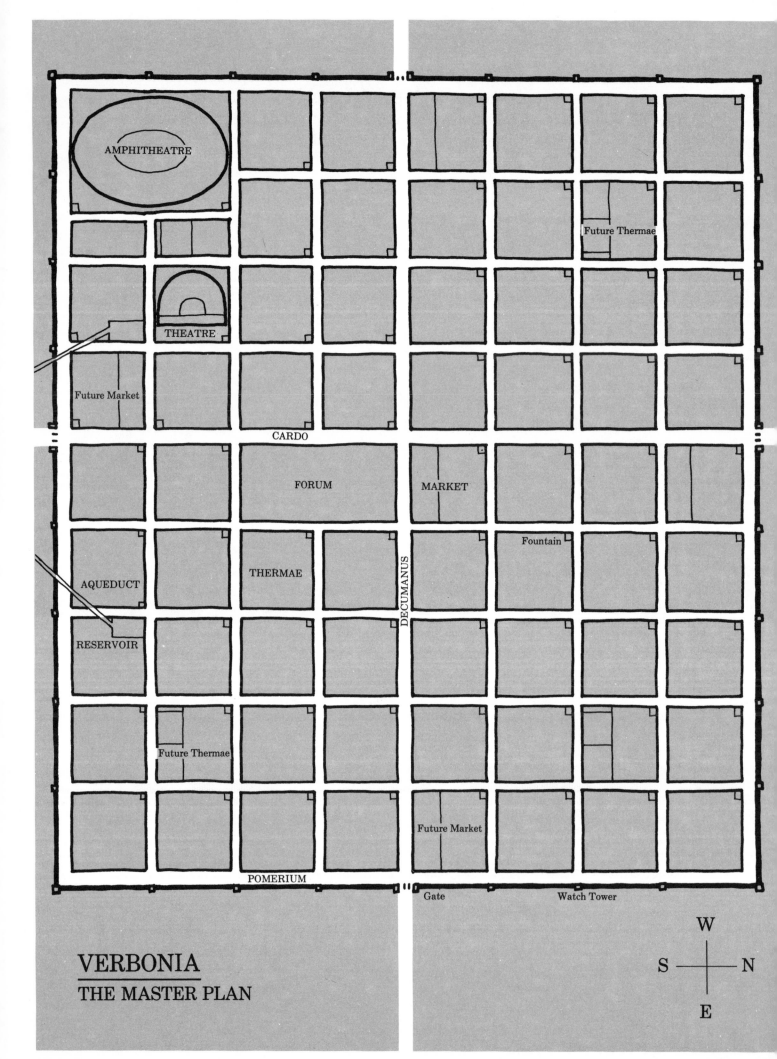

AMPHITHEATRE

Future Thermae

THEATRE

Future Market

CARDO

FORUM

MARKET

Fountain

AQUEDUCT

THERMAE

DECUMANUS

RESERVOIR

Future Thermae

Future Market

POMERIUM

Gate

Watch Tower

VERBONIA
THE MASTER PLAN

W
S — N
E

The engineers worked throughout the winter measuring, designing, and drawing. By the spring of 25 B.C. (the Roman year 728) the master plan for Verbonia was ready. The centre of the castrum became the centre of the city. The main street running from north to south was now called the cardo, the one from east to west, the decumanus. Both were widened and lengthened and the rectangular area of the camp was increased to seven hundred and twenty yards long by six hundred and twenty yards wide. This space allowed a maximum population of approximately 50,000. A greater number, the planners believed, would make the city too large and unable to meet the needs of the people.

The entire area was divided by roads into a chessboard pattern. Almost all of the blocks, called insulae, were eighty yards square. A high wall was designed around the city in which fortified gates were located where the main streets cut through. Around the city but inside the wall a thirty-foot-wide strip of land called the pomerium was marked off. It represented the sacred boundary of the city within which the land was protected by the gods.

The city planners indicated those facilities which served all the residents. They designed a new and larger forum which was to become the government and religious centre of the city. They located public water fountains, the aqueduct that would bring the water, a central food market, public baths and lavatories, and an entertainment centre made up of a theatre and amphitheatre. They also set aside spaces for future buildings.

No privately owned building, they decreed, could be higher than twice the width of the street on which it stood. This insured that sunlight always reached the streets. They also required all persons whose buildings faced one of the main streets to build, at their own expense, shelter over the pavement for the comfort and protection of all pedestrians.

TYPICAL INSULA

The master plan allowed much freedom for the residents to determine the appearance and character of the city through the buildings they would construct for themselves. Each insula, left deliberately empty on the plan, would eventually be filled with buildings of all sizes and be crossed by narrow back roads and alleys.

Some of the insulae designated for private ownership were divided up among the soldiers, traders, and farmers. The names of the owners and the sizes of their holdings were inscribed on the plan and sent to the land office in Rome. A copy of the plan was carved on marble and stood in the forum for everyone to see. Even though land was given to Verbonia's first settlers, each person had to pay for the construction of his own house.

In the early summer of 25 B.C. a plough drawn by a white cow and a white bull guided by a Roman priest cut a furrow around the site. This solemn religious ceremony marked the location of the city wall and insured further protection by the gods. The plough was lifted only where gates were to be built.

Following the ceremony the surveyors marked off the roads using an instrument called a groma to make certain that all roads intersected at right angles. The groma was a pole about four feet high on top of which a cross was laid flat. When weighted strings hanging from each end of the cross hung parallel to the centre pole the groma was known to be perpendicular to the ground. The streets could be accurately marked off by sighting down the intersecting arms of the cross.

The same method was used to mark off roads and farmland outside the city.

The materials used most in the construction of Verbonia were stone, clay, mortar, and wood. The stone came from a limestone quarry owned by the government. Besides many work sheds, the quarry contained a forge for making and repairing tools and a carpenter's shop in which cranes and pulleys were built.

The skilled labourers cut, polished, or carved inscriptions in the stone. The unskilled workers separated and lifted the huge blocks from the earth. The stone was usually cut with a saw. When the stone was very hard, the blade used in the saw had no teeth; sand and iron filings were placed under the blade and the back-and-forth motion of the saw ground away the stone.

When the stone could not be sawed, a row of holes was drilled where it was to be divided. Wooden stakes were then jammed into the holes. When water was poured over the stakes, they swelled, splitting the stone along the line of holes.

The clay was made into bricks and tiles in factories near Arretium. The clay, dug out of large pits in the ground, was formed into standard shapes and sizes using wooden moulds. The mould was then removed and the wet clay placed in an oven to dry and harden. All bricks and tiles were stamped with the name of the factory owner and the name of the Emperor.

The mortar used between bricks and stones and in concrete was a mixture of sand, lime (a powder obtained by burning limestone), and water. When mortar was used in construction underwater, a gravelly substance called pozzolana was added which made the mortar become extremely hard when it set.

The wood used for scaffolding and roof framework came from a forest at the foot of the Apennine mountains to the south.

Before building could begin, labourers had to be found. Besides the soldiers many poor farmers from the countryside came to work and settle in the city. The majority of workers however were slaves, either owned by the state or by wealthy businessmen, or they were prisoners of war from Gaul, Greece, or Egypt. Unless they were skilled, the labourers were formed into work gangs to do jobs requiring no particular skill. To maintain as high a level of work as possible the labourers were treated almost as well as the soldiers.

Saw

Compass

Pattern

Hammer

Measuring Stick

Chisel

Pattern

Pickaxe

Square

Drill

STONEWORKING TOOLS

Axe

Auger

Sledge Hammer

Wedge

Spansaw

Axe

Plane

Pincers

A great variety of tools was needed throughout the construction of the city. Most were made in forges and workshops on the site. The more precise measuring instruments and squares were brought from Rome.

The new roads and bridge were completed before work began on the city itself. Once the surveyors had marked out a road with stakes, a ditch was dug on each side into which a row of kerbstones was set. A deeper ditch was then dug between the two rows of kerbstones which was filled with layers of stones of varying size. The top layer formed the surface of the road and rose slightly in the centre to force the rainwater into the side ditches. The paving was constructed of flat stones that were carefully fitted together. Any spaces left between them were filled with smaller stones or pieces of scrap iron.

From the boat bridge work began on the permanent bridge. It was to be made of wood and supported on five stone towers called piers which were to stand in the river. Cofferdams were built so the labourers could erect the piers without having to work underwater. First, piles were driven into the riverbed. These were oak tree trunks, with all the bark scraped off, chiselled to a point at the bottom. They were chained together vertically in a shape around which the river could easily flow. When the gaps between the piles had been filled with clay, the water was pumped out of the enclosed area.

Each pier stood on a foundation of tar-covered piles and was constructed of carefully cut stones on the outside and smaller uncut stones on the inside. The mortar used between the stones contained pozzolana. When the piers reached a height of thirty feet above the river, wooden arches were hoisted into place between them.

A wooden road was nailed to the arches and covered with a layer of earth. The finished road stood almost sixty feet above the river.

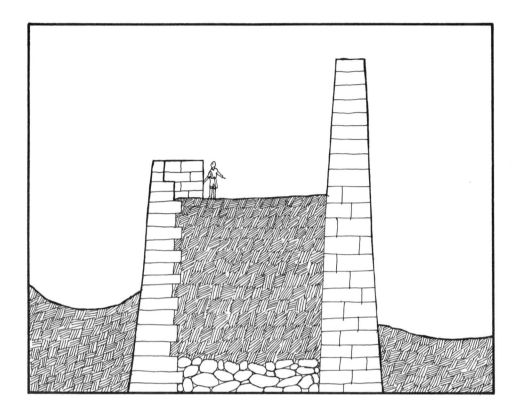

The city wall was built next. Two large ditches were dug along the furrow and the earth was heaped into a high mound between them. A stone wall was built against each side for additional strength. The base of the outer wall went down thirty feet below ground level, making it almost impossible for anyone to tunnel under. On top of the outer wall alternating high and low sections called crenellations were built. The soldiers were protected behind the high sections while firing their weapons over the low sections. The inner wall was several feet higher than the outer wall to block the path of rocks and arrows that might be fired into the city.

Cranes on top of the mound lowered the stones into place. Four men standing inside a wooden wheel at the base of the crane provided the power. As they walked forward the wheel turned, rotating an axle which wound the rope. The engineers constantly checked to make sure each course of stones was level.

The stones were locked together by I-shaped iron clamps which fit into precut grooves. Molten lead poured over each connection sealed the clamps permanently.

Each gate contained three vaulted openings, one for the road and another for each pavement. When the walls on both sides of the road were finished, a wooden arch called a centering was supported between them on projecting stones. The masons, working from both sides, then placed wedged-shape stones on top of the centering. When the keystone was inserted in the centre, the arch was complete. The centering was then moved sideways and another arch was constructed next to the first. This process was repeated until the entire passage-way was covered by a semicircular roof called a tunnel vault. The pavements were covered in the same way.

The openings in the gate were sealed by heavy wooden doors. The central opening was also protected by a wooden grate called a portcullis, lowered from a room above the street. Both the doors and the portcullis were covered with bronze plates.

Along the wall and on each side of the main gates high watchtowers were built for additional protection.

At first, Verbonia's drinking water came from several deep wells within the city walls. But the planners knew that as the population increased the wells would no longer be sufficient. A pipeline called an aqueduct was proposed to bring water from the mountain lakes thirty-eight miles to the south.

When the best route for the aqueduct had been chosen, a profile map of the land was drawn showing the hills and valleys. To determine the profile, surveyors used levelling instruments called chorobates. The chorobate was known to be level when weighted strings fastened to the horizontal bar hung parallel to the legs. This was double-checked by pouring water into a groove on top of the horizontal bar. When the distance between the top of the water and the top of the bar was the same all around the groove, the instrument was level.

By sighting along the chorobate the surveyors were able to create an imaginary horizontal line over the entire route of the aqueduct. Every forty feet along this line the vertical distance between it and the ground was recorded. When the line was drawn on parchment the vertical distances were marked below it. By connecting all the marks with a single line the mapmakers obtained an accurate profile of the land. By then drawing the line of the aqueduct on the plan the engineers could easily see whether it would sit on the ground, cut through the ground, or rise above the ground.

The aqueduct had to be built with a constant slope from beginning to end to keep the water moving.

To prevent people from stealing or poisoning the water, most of the aqueduct was raised about fifty feet off the ground. It was supported by a continuous row of arches built on tall square piers which rested on deep foundations.

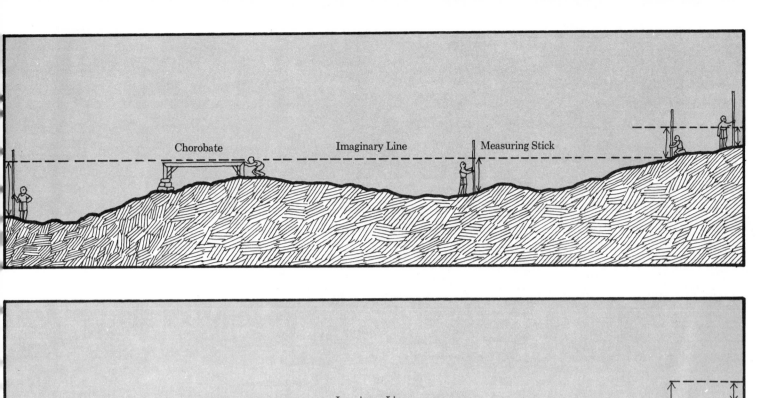

Chorobate   Imaginary Line   Measuring Stick

Imaginary Line

PROFILE MAP

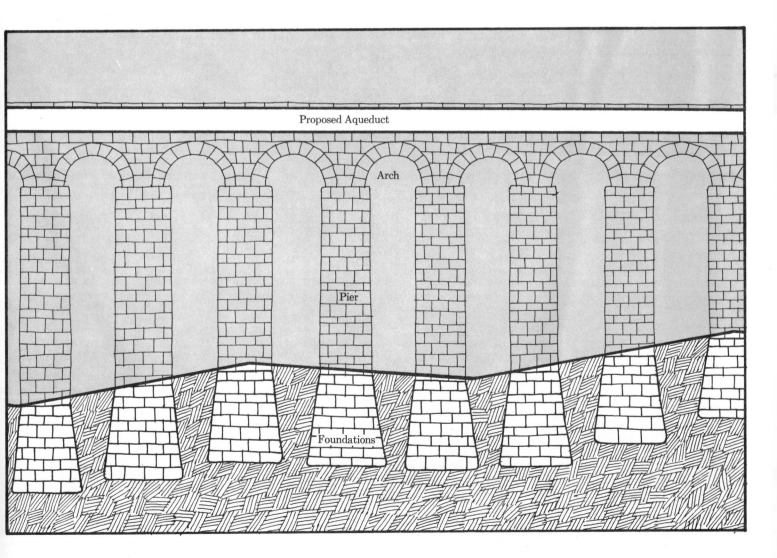

Proposed Aqueduct

Arch

Pier

Foundations

The foundations and piers were constructed of stone-faced concrete — stone set in mortar on the outside with layers of concrete on the inside. To make the concrete, the masons first laid a course of rough stones across the area to be filled. The mortar men then covered the stones with a layer of mortar to bind them together. When the mortar had set, the process was repeated.

When two piers were finished, an arch was constructed between them. The aqueduct, itself a rectangular stone pipe about four feet wide and six feet high, was then built on top. The inner surface of the pipe was lined with hard cement to prevent leaks.

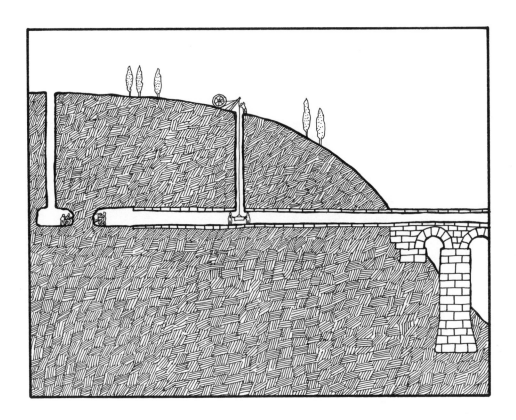

The route chosen for the aqueduct required that a short tunnel be dug through a hill. Every twenty yards vertical shafts were sunk from the surface of the hill to the level of the proposed aqueduct. The depths of the shafts were measured from the profile plan.

The labourers connected the ends of the shafts, and as a section was completed the masons lined it with stone and cement.

Appius Fluvius, the chief water engineer, rode out from the city once a week to inspect construction. The foremen and labourers lived in camp sites which moved with the aqueduct farther and farther from the city. For twenty miles the aqueduct ran alongside the main highway, and the labourers would often stop to watch the endless procession of merchants and farmers. About three years after construction began, large numbers of families could be seen travelling towards the city. Many belonged to the soldiers stationed in Verbonia. During the fifth year of construction the aqueduct turned away from the highway and two years later it was completed.

Before the wall of the city was finished, work began on the streets. Verbonia's streets were designed for people. Therefore adequate pavements were built and strict laws were written to control any movement of carts and chariots which could endanger the health and safety of people in the streets.

During the day all carts and chariots except those carrying building materials were banned from the streets. This meant that deliveries had to be made at night or in the early morning. Carts and horses were very noisy, so many of the streets on which people lived were made one way or dead end to reduce traffic.

The pavements on both sides of the streets were raised one and a half feet above the road surface. This precaution prevented vehicles from accidentally rolling into the path of pedestrians. Steppingstones were embedded in the middle of the road to connect the pavements. Animals and carts could straddle the stones — but only if they went slowly. In this way the stones helped to enforce the speed limit. When it rained, the streets were the gutters through which water ran into sewers under the pavements. The steppingstones enabled people to cross the street without getting their sandals drenched. The cardo and decumanus were finished first. Other streets were completed as the area around them developed.

In 20 B.C. Appius and his staff started on the supply system that would distribute water throughout the city. The aqueduct was carried over the south wall and connected to two reservoirs. These were deep rectangular pools whose walls were brick-faced concrete — a wall of triangular bricks on the inside and outside enclosing layers of concrete. Every few feet the top of the wall was covered with three courses of large flat bricks. This allowed the contractor to adjust the level of the wall if it was not perfect.

Each reservoir was covered by a concrete tunnel vault. The vaults were constructed over a semicircular wooden form supported on scaffolding between the sides of the pool. Brick reinforcing arches were first constructed over the form ten feet apart. The entire form was then lined with flat bricks and covered with a thick layer of concrete. When the concrete hardened and could stand by itself the form was moved into the next position. Using the same form over and over, the process was repeated until the reservoir was covered. The brick facing on the inside surface of the vault and walls was covered with hard cement. The outside of the vault was shaped like a pitched roof and covered with tiles.

1

2

3

4

5

6

On the wall at one end of the reservoir were several gates channelling the water into lead pipes which ran either to public fountains, lavatories, and baths, or to the homes of the wealthy. When there was a shortage of water, the gate leading to these homes was closed, and then, if necessary, the gate to the baths and lavatories was closed as well. This insured that the public fountains supplying the majority of Verbonia's residents would be the last to run dry. The water for wealthy homes was first piped into a lead tank placed on one of many high brick towers. As it ran back down other pipes, the water gained enough pressure to feed all the houses to which the tower was connected.

In order for the water supply system to be efficient, an equally efficient drainage system was required. Sewers originally constructed under the sidewalks for rainwater were enlarged. They were connected to both public and private buildings by clay pipes. Some of the sewers were six feet deep. They were all built of stone and mortar and their tops were removable stone slabs in case repairs were necessary. The slabs were covered by compressed earth in which the lead supply pipes from the water towers were laid.

All the sewers were connected to two cloacae — tunnels large enough to walk in — which carried the water under the walls of the city and down to the river. Iron grills were installed inside them which let the water out but prevented anyone from getting in.

By 19 B.C. the city walls were finished and work began on the first and most important public areas of the city — the forum and the market.

THE FORUM · PLAN

The forum was paved and covered two entire blocks. At one end the temple of Jupiter, Juno, and Minerva was built. Of all the temples to be built in the forum this was the most important. At the opposite end, facing the temple, was the rostrum. This was a raised platform from which speeches were made and decrees were read to the residents of the city. Along one side of the forum stood the Curia — the building in which the elected senators of the city met. Next to the Curia was the Basilica, the court of justice. The temple was constructed of polished limestone, while the other two buildings were brick-faced concrete covered with sheets of limestone. All the roofs were made of triangular wooden frames called trusses, covered by rows of clay tiles.

The buildings and the forum were surrounded by rows of columns called colonnades. The columns were either built of cylindrical stone blocks set on top of each other or they were constructed of brick and mortar covered by cement.

A long two-story structure enclosed on both sides by colonnades was built to separate the forum from the busy streets. On the lower level were little shops which faced the street. On the second level were offices and schoolrooms which faced the forum.

Over the main entrance to the forum, off the cardo, a large triumphal arch was constructed to the glory of the Emperor. It was made of brick-faced concrete and covered with sheets of coloured marble. On special holidays processions would enter the forum through the arch.

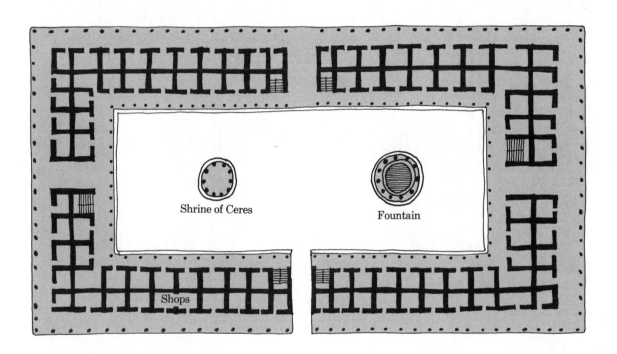

Shrine of Ceres

Fountain

Shops

THE CENTRAL MARKET · PLAN

Because new temples were always being enlarged or replaced the forum really wasn't finished for two hundred years. But the central market across the street was finished in less than five. This was not surprising since Verbonia's main function was that of a trading centre.

The open area in which farmers and merchants set up their stands covered almost half a block and was surrounded on all four sides by colonnades similar to those of the forum. In the centre was a public fountain and a shrine to Ceres, the goddess of agriculture.

Many of the offices on the second level were rented by businessmen who kept similar offices in other cities, including Rome. These men bought much of the produce from the fields around the city and shipped it to markets all over the empire.

Warehouses, for storing grain, wine, and oil, were built along the streets close to the market. The wine and oil were stored in large clay pots called amphorae buried in the ground, which kept them cool. To prevent moisture from damaging the grain crop it was stored on a floor supported two feet above a lower floor by brick piers. Ventilation holes in the raised floor let air move freely around the sacks of grain. Some of the larger warehouses contained many storerooms located around an open courtyard. Since much of the crop was transported by boat, a dock and some warehouses were constructed along the riverbank.

At first everyone shopped in the central market but as the population increased, the market, in spite of its size, became too small. In anticipation of this, the planners had set aside areas on the master plan for future markets. Although they looked very similar, one market specialized in fruit and vegetables, another in grain, and a third, near the north gate and closest to the river, sold only fish.

Along the streets that connected the markets, shops and workshops were built side by side. On one street Marcus Licinius, who came from Rome, built a bakery. Bread was one of the most important foods for the people of Verbonia and many bakeries were built throughout the city. The main ingredient in the bread was flour, which was obtained by grinding grain in stone mills. Each mill consisted of two main pieces. The outer piece was rotated around the inner piece by pushing on the projecting arms. The grain was crushed or milled as it passed through the narrow space between the two. The flour that came out at the bottom of the mill was mixed with water and made into dough. Salt and leaven were then added. The dough was kneaded and formed into flat circular loaves and baked in a large brick oven.

THE HOUSE OF MARCUS LICINIUS • PLAN

The contractor who built Marcus' bakery also built his house. Like those of his neighbours, Marcus' house was quite large. The exterior walls were brick-faced concrete. Some of the interior walls were the same, while others were vertical wooden frames filled with small stones and mortar. All the walls were covered with a thick coat of plaster called stucco and painted.

There were many areas shown on the plan but two were much larger than the others. The first, at the front of the house, was called the atrium and was connected to the pavement by a narrow passage. The second, in the rear of the house, was a garden surrounded by a colonnade. This area was called the peristyle. The dining room, library, kitchen, and storerooms were located around the atrium, while the bedrooms and servants' quarters were on a second level.

Most of the activities took place in the atrium because of its size and the light that came through a square opening in the roof. Under the opening, called a compluvium, a shallow pool, called an impluvium, was sunk into the floor. Rain which fell into the impluvium ran through a small hole and into an underground tank. When water was needed the cover was taken off the tank and a clay jug lowered into it.

Marcus' favourite part of the house was the peristyle. It was quiet and private and very relaxing after a few hours in the bakery. It contained a fountain which could be turned off and on by a tap. It also contained a shrine to the Lares — the gods who protected Marcus' house.

The floors of the atrium and peristyle were covered with mosaic — small black and white marble tiles that were pressed into wet cement in a variety of geometric patterns.

Because one house was built right up against another the only windows were located at the front facing the street. These were usually very small and covered with bars for security.

To brighten up the small dark rooms colourful pictures were painted on the walls. Many rooms contained jungle scenes full of wild animals and exotic plants. Imitation windows were painted in other rooms to make them seem less confining. In the winter the important rooms were heated by wood stoves.

On one side of the passage between the pavement and the atrium a lavatory was connected to the sewer pipe and flushed by a continuous stream of water. On the other side a room that opened onto the pavement was rented out to a jeweller named Lucius Julius, who knew that a jewellery shop in Marcus' neighbourhood would be very profitable.

Lucius was a former slave who had learned his craft in Egypt and had taken the name of the man who bought and eventually freed him. He and his family lived in an apartment in another section of the city.

Both the interior and exterior walls of this building were constructed of heavy timber framework filled with stone and mortar and covered with stucco. Instead of an atrium the apartment building contained a small courtyard above which was a high open space. It was called a light shaft because it supplied the only natural light for the small inner rooms.

The few rooms of Lucius' apartment were quite small and the same one was often used for many purposes. The largest of the rooms opened onto a balcony overlooking the street.

On the ground floor of the building was a shop which sold olive oil. Besides amphorae buried in the ground for storing the oil the shop contained a press for squeezing the oil out of the olives.

Some of the apartment buildings had small wells but few contained lavatories; most of the residents used the public lavatories located around the city.

All the buildings in Lucius' neighbourhood contained two or more apartments. Many were owned by Marcus Licinius' neighbours and all contained shops opening onto the pavement. One of those shops was rented by a barber named Quintus Aurelius. The success of Quintus' business was mostly due to his willingness to gossip. For spreading news Quintius and Verbonia's other barbers were almost as important as the government decrees read in the forum, and they were definitely faster.

By the time of Augustus' death in A.D. 14, the streets of Verbonia were lined with grocery shops, pastry shops, ceramic shops, furniture shops, clothing shops, apothecaries, wine shops, and eating places.

Many of the craftsmen on a particular street often specialized in the same or related crafts. Most of the shops along a small quiet street near the forum were owned by highly skilled gold workers and the street eventually became known as "the street of gold." The craftsmen and their families lived in rooms behind or above their shops. As neighbourhoods developed, families often got together to build shrines on their streets dedicated to the Lares.

Most of the eating places were owned by Servius Vitellius, who also owned a chain of them in Ariminum. They opened onto the pavement and each contained a concrete serving counter decorated with pieces of coloured marble. Clay jugs embedded in the counter contained hot and cold drinks to be sold. A row of clay drinking cups marked with Servius' name stood on a marble shelf next to the counter.

At night and during the hot afternoons all the shops could be closed by fitting wooden panels into grooves on the tops and bottoms of the doorways. A lock was used to secure them in place. At night the city provided torch-carrying watchmen who patrolled the streets checking the locks and doors of all the buildings.

Upon his death Augustus became a god, and the Emperor Tiberius who succeeded him ordered the building of temples in Augustus' honour throughout the empire. As usual the citizens of each city, not the Emperor, paid for these temples.

The wealthy of Verbonia managed to take advantage of the situation by either renting some of their slaves to the contractor building the temple or by contributing enough money to insure that their names would be carved in some prominent place in the building.

Numerius Septimius, who owned a lot of farmland, was the wealthiest man in the city. Not only did he contribute willingly to the new temple, but he paid for the entire construction of a new market. So that everyone would know of his generosity he commissioned a marble statue of himself holding a bust of Ceres. It was carved in the workshop of Titus Statius, the best and largest stone cutting shop in the city. When it was finished it was transported by cart to the new market and erected near the fountain.

As open land within the walls gradually disappeared, the importance of care-
ful planning became more and more evident — especially in two well-thought-

out ideas. The first was the street plan, which maintained order throughout, and the second was the setting aside of land for recreation and entertainment.

The public baths, called thermae, were not only for washing but also provided a place to meet, talk, exercise, gamble, and even read. Bathing was traditionally accomplished in three stages. First the Romans washed in hot water from a pool in the steamy caldarium. Then they relaxed in a warm-water pool in the tepidarium and finally ended the process with a dive into the cold-water pool of the frigidarium.

Steam Room

Water Tanks

Service Corridor

Pool

Steam Room

Pool

Pool

Pool

Changing Room

Lav.

Exercise Room

Swimming Pool

CALDARIUM

TEPIDARIUM

FRIGIDARIUM

PALAESTRA

THERMAE
PLAN

Several small thermae were built during the reign of Augustus, but by A.D. 42 the population had reached 30,000 and the existing facilities were inadequate. The new Emperor Claudius ordered that a much larger thermae be built near the forum on the site of the original baths. A professional demolition company was hired and the old structure, along with a few apartment buildings, was torn down.

The mosaic-covered stone floors of the caldarium, tepidarium, and steam rooms were supported two feet off the ground by brick piers, creating a space below the floor called a hypocaust. Hot gases from a furnace outside the building were piped into the hypocaust to heat the rooms. When the hypocaust was

FRIGIDARIUM

Drain to Cloaca

PALAESTRA

full, the gas went up flues — clay pipes in the walls — heating the walls, and out through vents in the vaults.

Suspended over the furnace were large bronze tanks in which water was heated for the baths. The hot water ran into the pool of the caldarium and the overflow, cooling as it went, was piped into the pool of the tepidarium.

The caldarium, tepidarium, changing rooms, steam rooms, exercise rooms, eating places, and lavatories all had tunnel-vaulted ceilings. The larger area of the frigidarium was covered by a series of groin vaults which are created when two tunnel vaults cross each other at a right angle. Each of the cold-water pools in the frigidarium was covered by a dome ceiling with a round opening in the top, called an oculus, to let light in.

During the construction of both the domes and the vaults, wooden shapes called coffers were fastened on top of the forms. When the concrete had set, the form and coffers were lowered, leaving indentations in the surface of the ceiling which lightened but did not weaken it. This allowed the supporting walls or piers to be somewhat thinner.

Next to the thermae, a grassed area containing a swimming pool was enclosed by a two-story colonnade. This area was called the palestra and was used for exercising and wrestling, among other things. Behind the second floor colonnade and over the entrance a library was built with a collection of scrolls for those who wished to read.

To supply the increased amount of water needed for the larger baths and growing population a second aqueduct was constructed directly on top of the first.

SEATING

POOL

ARENA

THE AMPHITHEATRE • PLAN

The last public area to be fully developed was the city's entertainment centre. In A.D. 44 the senate voted to build a more permanent amphitheatre and theatre. Until that time a sloped earth mound lined with stone seats and reinforced by a ring of arches had enclosed both the arena and the stage of the theatre.

The original oval shape of the amphitheatre was maintained and enlarged. The stone seats now rested on two layers of tunnel-vaulted passages radiating out from the centre. These passages were connected by other passages which ran around the arena.

1

2

3

CONSTRUCTION OF
THE AMPHITHEATRE

4

Masts for Valarium

SEATING

ARENA

Water Supply Tunnel

THE AMPHITHEATRE SECTION

The arena was sunk several feet into the ground and surrounded by a high wall. Deep pools were built in the floor which could be filled for staging naval battles. When they weren't needed, they were covered by wooden boards and emptied through a canal into the cloaca.

Besides lavatories and an eating place the passages contained ramps and stair-

Animal Storage Room

Lava-
tories

Foundations

Drains

Drain to Cloaca

ways which enabled the entire twenty thousand spectators to enter or leave the structure in less than ten minutes. Wild animals and equipment used in the performances were kept under the lowest seats in rooms which opened onto the arena. The most popular performances involved the deaths of either animals, slaves, or gladiators — men paid to fight each other.

Two rows of arches, one on top of the other, formed the exterior wall of the amphitheatre. This wall was constructed of carefully cut stones clamped together with iron and bronze pins. The passages and vaulting were all constructed of stone and concrete. A rope net was suspended above the entire seating area from wooden masts. If the sun was too hot a canvas roof called a valarium was drawn over the seating area. When it rained during a performance everyone took shelter in the passages.

During the construction of the amphitheatre some formwork was accidentally moved before the concrete in the vault had completely set, killing twenty-five slaves, their foreman, and a senator observing the work from the ground. The bodies of the slaves were taken on two carts to a field four miles outside the city and buried in a large pit. The bodies of the senator and foreman were cremated and the ashes sealed in urns. The senator's urn was placed in his elaborate family tomb, much closer to the city but still outside the walls as required by law. The foreman's urn was buried in a public but still respectable graveyard, where his family erected a tombstone in his memory.

THE THEATRE · PLAN

Because the senator had always enjoyed plays, his family donated a large sum
of money toward the construction of the new theatre. The seats were built
around a steep semicircular pit called a cavea. Like the seats of the amphitheatre they were supported by a network of concrete tunnels. A long wooden stage
was constructed across the diameter of the cavea. At both sides of the stage
rooms were built for changing and storing costumes.

A curtain could be raised from under the stage for scenery changes. Behind the stage the wall called the frons scaenae was covered with marble columns and architectural ornamentation. This wall reached the same height as the colonnade that was built around the last row of seats in the cavea. Sometimes the actors performed in the orchestra — the flat semicircular area directly in front of the stage. The most important people sat either on wide seats around the orchestra or in balconies over the side entrances. The theatre, too, could be covered by a valarium.

By A.D. 75 both the amphitheatre and theatre were finished and a festival which lasted twenty-five days was held to celebrate the occasion.

As Verbonia's population steadily climbed, most landlords replaced their small apartment buildings with large apartment blocks. Some, as high as five stories, contained twenty families. To take advantage of this height, which could still be no more than twice the width of the street, the senate passed a law limiting the first apartment blocks to insulae along the northern and western sides of the city. In the winter these buildings would shield the city from the cold wind that blew down the valley.

As in earlier buildings, the apartments in each block were built around a light shaft. The lowest level of the buildings was a series of tunnel-vaulted rooms built side by side and opening onto the pavement. These spaces were rented by shopkeepers who constructed a wooden platform on which to live eight feet above the floor. Stables and storerooms around the central courtyard were also rented out.

By A.D. 100 Verbonia's population was almost fifty thousand. Many of the insulae now contained up to eight large apartment blocks and only the wealthiest residents of the city could afford privately owned houses. As the demand increased, old thermae, markets, and temples were torn down and replaced by larger, more adequate structures. The two aqueducts still satisfied the city's

water needs and the one-hundred-and-twenty-year-old sewer system was still operating flawlessly. Because of the efficient organization of farmland and the large number of markets and bakeries, food continued to remain in good supply. The streets, although busy, were not overcrowded. They were still safe and comfortable outdoor areas as originally intended in the master plan.

One hundred and twenty-five years after its founding, Verbonia had reached its limit. With the empire stronger than ever the walls once constructed to keep the enemy out were now serving a more important function — that of keeping the city in.

GLOSSARY

AMPHITHEATRE
An oval arena completely surrounded by gradually rising rows of seats.

ATRIUM
The largest interior space in a Roman house. It is completely covered by a roof except for the central section which is left open to the sky.

AQUEDUCT
A pipeline specifically built to carry water.

AXLE
The shaft on which a wheel revolves.

CALDARIUM
The heated area of the thermae containing hot water pools.

CARDO
The main north-south road through a Roman city.

CASTRUM
A Roman military camp usually square or rectangular in shape.

CAVEA
The steep semicircular seating area of the theatre.

CENTERING
A temporary wooden arch over which a brick or stone arch is constructed. When the mortar sets between the bricks or stones of the permanent arch, the centering is removed.

CHOROBATE
A long wooden surveying instrument used for general siting as well as determining the profile of the land.

CLOACA
A large underground sewer in the form of a tunnel.

COFFERDAM
A water tight enclosure constructed in a river or lake. The water is pumped out of the cofferdam enabling labourers to work directly on the river or lake bed.

COFFERS
Recessed areas in a concrete vault or dome which reduce the weight of the roof.

COLONNADE
A row of columns supporting a horizontal beam or a roof.

COMPLUVIUM
The opening in the roof of the atrium.

CONCRETE
An extremely strong building material made by combining stones of varying sizes and mortar.

CRENELLATIONS
The alternating high and low sections of stonework along the top of a defensive wall. The defender is protected behind the high sections while firing his weapon over the lower sections.

DECUMANUS
The main east-west road through a Roman city.

FORGE
A workshop in which metal is heated in a furnace and hammered into shapes for tools and instruments.

FORUM
The government and religious centre of a Roman city consisting of an open meeting area surrounded by buildings and colonnades.

FRIGIDARIUM
The area of the thermae containing cold water pools.

GROIN VAULT
The vault created by the intersection of two tunnel vaults at right angles to each other.

GROMA
A surveying instrument consisting of a pole and a horizontal cross from which hang four weighted strings. When the strings hang parallel to the pole the instrument is known to be perfectly vertical and the roads and walls could then be accurately laid out on the ground by siting along the arms of the cross.

HYPOCAUST
The chamber under a raised floor into which hot gases were piped in order to heat the floor.

IMPLUVIUM
The pool in the floor of the atrium which collected the water that fell through the compluvium.

INSULA
A Roman city block, usually square or rectangular in shape.

KEYSTONE
The central locking stone at the top of an arch.

MORTAR
A mixture of sand, lime and water used to cement stones and bricks together. When it dries it becomes very hard.

OCULUS
A round opening or window.

PERISTYLE
The open courtyard or garden in a Roman house surrounded by a colonnade.

PIERS
A free-standing brick, stone or concrete structure similar to a column but usually thicker, used to support an arch.

PILE
A tree trunk stripped of bark and pointed at one end that is then driven into a river bed or marshy area in the construction of a cofferdam or is used to create a sturdy base for a pier.

POMERIUM
The open strip of land along the inner face of the wall around a Roman city. It served as the sacred boundary within which the land was thought to be protected by the gods.

PORTCULLIS
A metal-clad timber grill which could be lowered to seal off the gates of the city.

POZZOLANA
A gravelly substance mixed with regular mortar, enabling it to harden under water.

PROFILE MAP
A drawing which outlines the surface of the land showing the height and depth of hills and valleys.

ROSTRUM
A raised platform from which speeches are delivered.

STUCCO
Heavy plaster.

TEPIDARIUM
The heated area of the thermae containing hot water pools.

THERMAE
Roman public baths.

TRUSS
A wooden frame used to bridge a space too wide to be bridged by a single beam.

TUNNEL VAULT
A continuous semicircular ceiling or roof.

VALARIUM
A canvas roof drawn over a theatre or amphitheatre to protect the spectators from the sun.